I0190974

THE ABSENCE
OF COLOR

A MISFIT'S BOOK
OF POETRY

The Absence of Color

A Misfit's Book of Poetry

By
Myrica Cook

Copyright © 2019 by OffBeat Publishing
All rights reserved.
This book or any portion thereof may not be reproduced
or used in any manner whatsoever without the express
written permission of the publisher except for the use
of brief quotations in a book review.

Printed in the United States of America

First Printing, 2019

OffBeat Publishing

ISBN: 978-1-950464-04-3

*This book is dedicated to all the Misfits
who dance to their own beat.*

TABLE OF CONTENTS

Forward

Two things about the beginning of my life led to my being a misfit. I was an only child, and I lived under a roof in which existence was dark. This combination led to me being an introvert with only a handful of friends at any given time. Even now, near the age of fifty, I have a mere handful of those I consider friends. I don't say this to complain or because I seek pity; I say this because it makes my knowing the author of this poetry collection that much more special.

Although her background is vastly different, Myrica Cook's childhood is not lacking in its own versions of darkness and despair. I think this is why the title, *The Absence of Color* is so fitting.

Take her poem, *Only Silence Remains*. Only someone with a personal history of pain could visualize such scenes of anguish. This is the oldest poem in the collection, written when Myrica was eighteen. In *Voice*, she is possibly struck by fear of harsh truth, and can no longer sing her song.

Consider disregarding any philosophies you may have about poetry. While Myrica does have formal education in writing, (in which her talent has grown over the years), she has many times abandoned mainstream styles. In the case of poetry, I prefer this. The default should be the spilling out of the soul.

In the pages ahead there are scattered some hopeful or bright spots. This is of course the nature of darkness. Make no mistake, the depths of blackness run deep. Read in silence, and read to be a part of the emotions which were and are still so real in this author I've come to love. I'm happy to include this book on my bookshelf, and proud to include this Misfit poet as a friend.

Robert Kimbrell,
Author

Acknowledgement

I would like to acknowledge Mark Kinsey for his partnership in several poems written during our college days at Emory & Henry College. We would commute to his parent's house in Nitro, West Virginia, which was about three hours from college. We rarely listened to music because we were too busy writing about duck ponds and the open road. Thank you, Mark, for the car rides and the memories of a special time.

Included at the end of the College Years portion of the book is a poem entitled, *Moving ahead, always 1 step behind*, which is one of our fun collaborations.

College Years

Only Silence Remains

Trapped,
>within a wall of endless pain
>a life inside a barricade of twisted metal wire,
>sharp knives cutting flesh in two

She tries to see beyond reality,
>block out the horror around her.

Tears overspill to the dirt floor,her home of no warmth.

Bodies push together,
>sweat upon skin,
>skin upon bones.

No sleep here.
No joy here.
Just tears.
No hope here.
No freedom here.
Just more tears.
No food here.
No sun here.
Just tears soaking the ground to dry for eternity

She tries to block out the screams,
>"No! Not me! Don't take me!
>Scream upon scream
>Wife, mother, woman
>Husband, father, man
>Innocent, pure, child

LOUDER

LOUDER it grows,
>pounding away at her ears like drums
>"Not me! Not me!"

Stop daydreaming! Get to work you good for nothing trash!

Her callused hands can feel the dirt
icy and hard beneath her fingertips,
bloody and raw from digging

Move away, move away, here's another load!

One by one,
        dropping into the pit of darkness,
        skeletons being fed a new
        batch of shaven tattoos.

Hey, you! Come here! It's your turn to die!

Fear,
        enclosing her soul,
        her heart beating quickly as her
        face grew paler in the light

A hand,
        rough from torture and murder
        pushed her to her doom.

The screams were coming back,
        she could smell the blackened flesh
        burning inside the fiery ovens,
        corpses of ash left on the floors.

Go on... There isn't room for another Jew like you!

Scream upon scream,
        louder and louder.
Where did it come from?
Whose voice could be so piercing?
He gagged her with his fist,
        the screams were finally stopped.
The screams were hers…

The Untouchable One

We all have that one love
That untouchable being
That sears his heat into your soul
That unthinkable lover that touches
You like other
Dreaming of this over and over
With each breath
Of your Live
You would give up the world around you
For one last chance to feel
Whole once again

Change

"Change," he whispered in her ear.

"Why?" she asked.

"For me," he said so sweetly

"For what reason?"

"Because I'll love you more," he promised.

"No, you don't love me enough," she said as she walked away.

Another Man's Poetry

Death is to you a Dark Angel

Life has a two-faced lover,
No one is safe
In its hands anymore

A beginning…
Becomes an end

The love you speak of
Are only ghosts to me
Existing in your fantasy
With which you like to play

I am not among them

I am the Torn
The Wounded
The Angel of Death
Whom you love so dearly

Find yourself,
My dearest one

And do not hide beyond
The gates this time
For the Angel you wish
To keep
Wants to be set free

Ode to Rilke: A Bit of Advice

Take the difficult road before you,
the easy is too simple

Difficult is solitude
Difficult is loving

Take the lessons as they come,
for to learn within maturity,
means to love within reality

Men and women shed your past
change the experiences that you're known,
Because...

Difficult is solitude
Difficult is loving

Be aware of a transition,
inside your sadness,
from it grows the future.

Arrange your life according
to the ruling counsel,
then you'll find the difficult
upon which to hold
not so foreign after all.

The Chase

He runs
Screaming into the cold
Night air
They chase
No sound falls from his lips,
He only hears his heart
Pumping in his ears
They chase on
He is full of fear,
Surrounded by unknown
Voice
They chase
He feels faint,
Weariness clutches at
His legs
The chase on
He drops,
Hiding behind a wall of stone
They chase
Hidden for now
They chase on
Trapped
They chase
He looks up,
Pools of terror in his eyes
They chase no more
One man caught in the line
Of many
One down….

YOU to go

Becoming

I was still a child
I kept my innocence
I lost my innocence
I stayed alone
I remained with others
I lost myself
I fell in love
I fell out of love
I learned to hate
I feel in love again
I gave up on life
I lost Faith
I found God
I have gained strength
I learned to take
I learned to give
I love with pain
I have endured
I became a sister
I became a brother
I became an individual
I have known tears
I can still smile
I have forgiven others
I have forgiven myself
I decided to grow up
I remain a girl
I became a woman

Short
but
Sweet

Emory Bound

4 more days until I'm home
Where I can breathe the fresh air in
Where my mind can clear among
The gold falling leaves
Remembering the dreams
We all held so dear
Of our innocence and joy
4 more days until I'm home
Back in the arms of Emory Proud

Tea Time

Sun shining
Drinking tea
Getting ready for the
Long day ahead
But it's okay
Because you'll be home
To greet me

Reflections

Reflections of you and me
Kisses and laughter
Sunshine on our faces
Wind blowing through our hair
A beautiful day

Thoughts

Early morning silence
Wrapped inside the darkness
Moonlight cracking through
The curtains of my heart

Stick with ME

So many changes
Some rushed, some slow
All waiting to be layered
With patience and anticipation
Stick with me, darling
The best is yet to be

Daydreams

I had a poem on the tip of my tongue
But it was gone in an instant
As my thoughts lay with you
I dream of your kisses and your lips so divine
My poem would never capture this feeling inside

Snow Day

The night is quiet
As snow blankets the land
Hiding the ice that lies beneath
Keeping its secrets
Until the thaw begins

A Phantom Touch

Fingertips caressing my cheek
Soft and tender
Tickling my lips into a smile
Waking up in the dark
And finding no one there

Night Shift

It's 3am and I'm stuck in this dark hole
The patients keep trickling in
Seeking kind words and strong drugs
When will this night end
And I finally see my bed

Migraines

Staying awake as the minutes tick by
Dark sweetness in the absence of light
Cool sheets on my skin
And no pain in my head
This is bliss to a fault
Soon I'll drift into a dream

Words

Words whisper on the wind
Blowing past me
Keeping their hidden meaning
No one listens to mine in return
As they swirl in the breeze
On their way to the sea

Morning Kisses

The light hits your face
Softening your lips
Your smile says come hither
To kiss you good morning
Again and again and again

Love in
Many
Forms

Bliss

Your hands when soft leave a trace of warmth
Your hands when passionate leave a trail of heat and bruises
Your eyes when blue and caring fill me with love like no other
Your eyes when fiery and determined fills me with lust
Your lips so gentle on mine with small kisses
Your lips so hard when they crash against mine
Leaving me breathless and wanting
Your arms so nurturing and sweet
As they hold me close to your heart
Yet your arms enclose me and hold me down tight
So the world becomes only you and me
Bliss is what takes us away and will always remain
Your parts all mean love to me

A Country Song

Standing at the kitchen sink
Country playing on my cell phone
Hips swaying to Keith Urban
On another late night, wide awake
Thinking of you night
Sleep eludes me as I remember
Your kissable lips on mine
Arms holding me tight
As we danced to Tim McGraw
Next to the sink in the kitchen
In a room full of boxes

The Quiet Space

Some say the silence
Between two people
Can be deafening
To us the silence
Is where our hearts lay
I hear your thoughts
As you hear mine
No words needed
Stay there in the silence
In love with me

Letting Go

Letting go of all the memories
Of you and I
Water falling from my eyes
No turn off valve
Until the well runs dry
Hands clutch my heart
Squeezing tighter and tighter
Until the dam bursts open
Letting us find our own
Paths to the ocean free

Lips

I miss his lips
When he isn't kissing me
So strong and so tender
His wicked way of
Making my tongue dance
When he crushes
My open mouth to his
His breath giving me life
And then makes me die
Each time he pulls away

The Drive

Driving in the night
Wishing the streetlights
Led me straight to you
The oncoming cars
Bright and harsh
Assaulting my eyes
Bouncing off my tears
Until I am nearly blind
Yet I keep driving
Towards the full moon
And away from you

Love is...

Sweet
Kind
Wild
Warm
Loud
Crazy
Obsessive
Kinky
Sizzling
Understanding
Amazing
Sad
Hurtful
Inspiring
Love is...life

A New Year

He spoke to me
Of Christmas gifts
To wish me well
He was once my love
But now a stranger
By New Year's Eve
A whisper might he be
No need for gifts
Or thoughts of old
As now two lovers
Beginning their year apart
With no more hands to hold

Goodbye

When all the
Goodbyes are done
And your hugs have
All been given
You give that one last kiss
While holding back your tears
Until you close the door behind you

Sunday

I miss you most on
Sunday afternoons
When I'm washing my face
To endure the long night ahead
Turning towards the mirror
In my nakedness
Pain strikes within
My body aching in need
I miss you most on Sunday afternoons

Evolving

Ode To A Silver Bullet

Shiny silver vessel
Reflecting the sun
All its hidden nooks
And crannies
Holding precious items
Sleek and modern
A stand out against
The large pop out
RVs lined up around us
Unique and beautiful
Windows darkened
From the outside stares
Running around naked
With families passing by
No one knows the wiser

Brain Dead

Tall belly and limbs
Splayed out for all to see
Gowned for privacy
Hidden under nothing
A naked shell of the large man he used to be
The steady clicking of the machines
Loud and echoing
His breath granted only by tubes
Legs twitching at the slightest touch
Seeing inside behind his eyes
There is nothing that stirs
In his state he is returned back home
Until his last breath is unplugged at the wall

Waiting

Waiting for the ball
To drop
Anticipating
Expecting
The worst
Every day
So it's been
Each day since leaving
For the new adventure
Of my life

A Silenced Voice

My voice has been stolen
I don't even sing
I used to turn up the stereo
Reveling in the sound
Fast beats
Slow Melodies
Notes draped
Notes layered
An aria of splendor
Rise high to the sky
Falling back upon me
A blanket of truth
The words collide
Striking the heart with its meaning
I used to sing aloud
Until you came along
Now all I do is listen
Because my lips are paralyzed

Vodka

I am most free
After a shot or three
That sting that hits my
Throat so sweet
My stomach grows warm
And my psyche settles in
I'm safe and I smile
No pain touches me now
Pour me another
So I can see Mars

Becoming Queen

She dreams of fairy tales
And golden wings
Of gilded castles
And a crown upon her head
She closes her book
The pages silent now
Another chapter awaits
Her tomorrow
When she can be Queen again

Melancholy Thoughts

Moments of melancholy
Settle deep in my being
Sadness keeps washing over me
Not sure of the reason
Just a moment in time
But it aches and it twists
All the happiness inside
Hate of it permeates all that I am
Until it passes tomorrow
And sets me free

Heroin

I'm playing connect the dots
With the trail of needle marks
Up and down her skinny arms
She cries out fake tears
And clutches her chest
Releasing a piercing wail
That stabs at our ears
"Hold still, hold still."
We repeat over and over
"I can't, I can't!"
She moans
She moves
Over and over
Contempt fills us as she
Continues to scream
If we only had straps
To entomb the monsters
That ooze from the holes
In her arms

Renaissance

With flowing skirts held high
Dancing amongst the wildflowers
Blowing wishes to the gods
Hoping dreams do come true
As faeries light up the night sky
Leading my love to you

Chains

I have been held down
By your chains too long
They have made me
Burn and bleed
Cutting and sizzling
Into my flesh
Scarring my soul
Against the evil of you
Your wicked ways of
Taking my love
To glorify your Unholy name
Your words made me cry out
In pain and in fear
Your kisses now turn my heart black
Breaking the chains that
Kept me bound to you
Now is my time in the sun
Though I may love you
Til the end of my day

Oma

My heart is 800 miles away
In the town where I was born
Where cathedral spires
Rise high in the air
The castles remain
Still strong
So true
Resilient like her
This is where Oma now lies
Taking secrets to her grave

Alone

Relying on Self
Heart beating quickly
Brain fogging over
Decisions to be made
Fear encasing
To make the wrong move
No one to ask
No one to guide
Relying on Self
Alone

Cocktail of Drugs

A cocktail of oblong and square
Sometimes round and rectangular
All keep the shakes at bay
My mind often races
Even with the elixir of life
My vision goes fuzzy
Hands tremble at the smallest of tasks
Unable to focus on one person or thing
The voices around me
Become a ring in the ears
Only way to resolve this
Is to rock myself back and forth
Until sleep overtakes me
I'm blissfully unaware
Of the hell deep inside me
Until I awake for another cocktail

The White Dress

Her white dress billowed out around her
Pink pained toes in the Cool sand
The mist from the ocean
Blew through her curled hair
Feeling light as a feather
As free as a bird
She could have stood
This way for years
But the memories came back
Crashing through her body
She had to make them stop
She stepped forward
Towards the wet sand
Walking slowly with her
Head held high
The water steadily rising
Creeping up to cover
Her legs, her hips, her waist
The white dress she couldn't
Wait to wear floated all
Around her
The intricate lace now
Dancing on the ocean waves
Ever forward she walked
Until she felt the beach floor
Drop off beneath her feet
Closing her eyes
She let the weight of the dress
Finally pull her down
So all that was left was her
Veil on the whitecaps of the surf

The Whip

The whip
Cracks hard
Against my back
Across the dip
Of tender skin
Relentless and cruel
Never pausing
For one sweet
Second to
Catch my breath
A steady rhythm
Of unforgiving Pain
The welts
Break open
Blood releases
Bathing my body
In hot release
As the whip stops
To be cleaned

Beast

His sweet smile
Beguiling in Charm
His boisterous
Laugh fills a room
His soft lips
Kissing ever so
Passionately
A perfect man
Until the lights are turned off
His gnarly fingers
Grab you tightly
He snarls with disgust
His canines grow long
His eyes transform
Into slits of vile green
He sniffs at your neck
Wanting to kill you
This is the man you promised to love
You let him dig his
Claws into your flesh
His sniffing stops
As he sinks his fangs
Into your beating vein
He drinks and drinks
Until he is sated
His claws pull out
Of her softness
As her head rolls to the side
He lays her down
Waiting for the bleeding to stop
Then curls up next to her
His blood frenzy haze
Giving way to a slumber
In the morning he wakes
Feeling her stir
Her wounds have all healed
From the lick of his tongue

Wings

Standing in the middle of the field
Cold dirt beneath my feet
Gaze held upward to the sky
Snow blanketing the earth with freshness
A rebirth into innocence
Walking forward will leave a trail
Of footprints far behind me
So I open my wings to fly

Notes

Only Silence Remains holds a special place in my heart. Sitting in a hot lecture hall while in college, I was listening to a guest speaker talk about surviving her time in a German concentration camp. The speech took me back to living as a young teenager in Germany. My parents had taken me to one of these camps, which was desolate and void of any warmth. I was allowed to walk through the barracks, which contained nothing but rows of empty bunk beds left behind. My parents chose to not expose me to other places such as the gas chambers. The eerie silence surrounding the camp is something I will never forget.

An Ode to Rilke was written at Emory & Henry College after an assigned reading on poet, Rainer Maria Rilke (Dec. 4, 1875 to Dec. 29, 1926).

Emory Bound was created with joy before driving to Emory & Henry College in Emory, Virginia, for my 25th college reunion.

Migraines. Since I was 16 year old I have battled with the pain of migraines. Even now at 49, the pain is present every day. There are still really bad days that leave me with no energy, but I give thanks for the good days that let me live my life at peace.

Brain Dead was written one night during my third shift schedule as a MRI Technologist. The patient had been in a horrific motorcycle accident. His family wanted an MRI to see if there was any chance at all of a viable brain. He was not wearing his helmet, and the resulting brain injury was fatal.

Heroin was composed after a particularly long third shift at the hospital in Dayton, Ohio. It was common to perform MRI exams on two to three patients a night from the emergency room with possible spinal infections due to drugs. Patients were often still high or needing another fix, screaming in pain, and writhing in discomfort. The majority of exams were seldomly successful as more drugs were needed to calm the patient down.

My *Oma* (German Grandmother) passed away a few weeks before Christmas 2018 at 97 years old. She was an amazing, resilient, and feisty woman.

In tribute to Oma

www.ingramcontent.com/pod-product-compliance
Lightning Source LLC
Chambersburg PA
CBHW071737020426
42331CB00008B/2066

9 781950 464043